DARING TO LIVE THE LIFE YOU'VE DREAMED

I MARRIED ADVENTURE

{ Journal }

Published by W Publishing Group,
a Division of Thomas Nelson, Inc., P.O. Box 141000, Nashville, Tennessee, 37214.

Unless otherwise indicated, Scripture quotations are from the The Holy Bible,
New International Version (NIV). Copyright 1973, 1978, 1984, International Bible Society.
Used by permission of Zondervan Bible Publishers.

Other Scripture references are from the following sources:
The Message (MSG), copyright 1993. Used by permission of NavPress Publishing Group.

ISBN 0-8499-1744-1

Printed in Singapore
02 03 04 05 TWP 9 8 7 6 5 4 3 2 1

Photographs and drawings throughout the book by Luci Swindoll.

Pablo Picasso, "Weeping Woman," 1937, © 2002 Estate of Pablo Picasso/Artists Rights Society (ARS), New York.

Art direction and design: David Riley + Associates
Newport Beach, California

DARING TO LIVE THE LIFE YOU'VE DREAMED

I MARRIED ADVENTURE
{ Journal }

LUCI SWINDOLL

W Publishing Group™

www.wpublishinggroup.com

A Division of Thomas Nelson, Inc.
www.ThomasNelson.com

A Place to Keep Your Soul Alive

To know what you prefer instead of humbly saying Amen to what the
world tells you you ought to prefer, is to have kept your soul alive.
—Robert Louis Stevenson

There was a sculptor who worked in a gigantic warehouse. He was a very dedicated artist with lots of energy, but to relax between high levels of concentration, he roller-skated. With loud music playing, he skated all over the warehouse doing different things—cooking lunch, cleaning up, casting something, grabbing a beer from the fridge, welding, even playing a few tunes on his saxophone while weaving around his studio between work stations. As I read about him, I could see it all in my mind's eye. He said he was "dancing, working, and having a good old time."

He wrote about that day in his journal. That's probably why we know he had days like that.

I, too, have a studio. I turned the walk-in closet in my bedroom into an itsy-bitsy art studio. Took out the bars for hanging clothes, added corbels to hold up the shelves, painted the whole thing a wonderful "Matisse" yellow, changed sliding wooden doors into bifold louvered doors, and converted the whole thing into a wonderful workplace. Once I'm seated, it's standing room only for anyone else.

The other day I sat at my drafting table in there, writing, drawing, and fiddling with a Lego toy. I listened to music from "Cirque du Soleil" as I straightened books on a shelf. Even organized a bunch of new stickers while eating a candy bar. Above my head there's a fat little bear on a unicycle, balancing a long, metal bar while riding up and down a string that's fastened to either side of the studio. I played with that. I was alone, happy, contented, and thoroughly entertained, enjoying complete freedom of self-expression.

I wrote about that day in my journal, just as I have the many days I've enjoyed in my little two-by-four cubicle. As a matter of fact, I write about every day in my journal . . . every adventure, whether at home or far away. And, I've done that for years. Most people know where they were the day Kennedy was shot, the day the first human stepped on the moon, and how they celebrated Christmas last year. But I know where I was the day before Kennedy was shot and the week after the moon landing and what I did every Christmas the last forty years. It's all in my journal.

The gospel writer with whom I most identify is Luke. He kept a journal. It's called "Acts." And, isn't that what we do every day somewhere, alone or with somebody else . . . act? Well, this old saint was astute enough to capture all those acts in a journal. While Matthew, Mark, and John give us amazing insight into the life of Christ, Luke gives us detail. I love detail! I love knowing who went where, who came along, who sat by whom, what they ate, and where they went immediately following dinner. Luke gives us all that info. I just know he kept a journal.

During childhood I wish somebody had said to me these three loving words: "Please take notes." I often heard "I love you" or "I'm so sorry". . . the phrases most kids long to hear. But nobody ever said, "Write this down." And now that I'm up to my ears in years, I want to read what I did back in my prehistoric days that I haven't recorded anywhere.

I come from a long line of journal keepers. My mother, grandmother, aunts, and cousins kept little books in which they recorded time and events. Many are filled with pictures and drawings. In some, there are challenges or exercises or accounts of their hopes and dreams.

I scan these treasured volumes from time to time and get insight into my past— my heritage. I feel myself smiling right now just thinking about those little volumes tucked away in a cedar chest.

Besides God Himself, I have no more devoted friend or companion in my life than my journal. I take her everywhere I go, spend time with her, pour out my heart to her, share my burdens and cares, let her see me at my best and worst. I entrust my soul to her keeping. She guards my secrets and lovingly holds my heart. She knows all the dreams I ever dared to entertain.

Chapter divisions in the Bible
did not come until the 13th
Century; the verse divisions
came about 300 yrs. latr.

TMS: Topical Memory System

▭ = Promises.

▭ = Salvation Verses

▭ = Connecting or significant
words or phrases.

▭ = anthropopathisms. (feelings)

▭ = anthropomorphisms. (forms)

"The purpose of every believer is
to so live, a ____ ____trols
the life, a ____ ____ DAILY."

↘ Greek if's
Phil. 2:1 - if = (1st class condition)
and it is true
Gal. 3:21 - if = (2nd class condition)
and it is not true
I John 1:9 - if = (3rd class condition)
maybe it is true; maybe it's not
I Peter 3:14 - if = (4th class condition)
I wish it were true, but it's no

Stems of Hebrew verbs:
① Cal - meant simply "to do it."
② Ni-fel = Reflective action.... it was "done to them."
③ Hith-pa-el - Had to it themselves and no
one else could do it for them. Lev. 5:5

When I go back to her years later, she's not forgotten a single word. She never filters through my musings, correcting grammar or spelling or editing my honest outpourings. She lets me rant and rave, praise and sing, cry and laugh, giving as much or as little detail as I want . . . from my own perspective without interrupting. She reflects where I've come from, where I am, and where I want to go. As I look back, I can see how I've changed and grown.

Emerson observed, "The unrecorded life is not worth examining." Why, then, do most of us shy away from recording our lives? Is it too hard? Too time consuming? Too boring? Perhaps that's how you feel. But the private contemplation that journaling provides gives us a place to examine what life really means to us. Within the covers of our own diary we can be mindful, playful, tearful, or awful. The paper doesn't care. It receives the mood we're in and preserves it for us to look at and learn from. Nothing can take the place of that and nobody can take it away from us. Every time we chronicle our thoughts and activities we are verifying our existence and silently thanking God we're alive.

I hope this adventure journal will be a place for you to keep your soul alive, as Stevenson says. On these pages you can record the life you're living as well as the life you want to live. There's room for both.

On occasion, I have opportunity to be with women, young and old, single and married, mothers and grandmothers, who ask me questions. They want to know the secret of my life or how I manage to enjoy it so fully. They want my advice. I hate giving advice and I'd never give it if I weren't coerced. I have a lot more questions than answers about life. But when I'm coerced, regardless of who asks, I always say, "My best advice is to keep a journal." It can be in a casual or an intense style, but "write it down."

Joan Didion says, "I write entirely to find out what I'm thinking, what I'm looking at, what I see, and what it means." That's what this journal is about. As you write, you'll be figuring yourself out. "People travel," Saint Augustine wrote, "to wonder at the height of the mountains, at the huge waves of the seas, at the long course of the rivers, at the vast compass of the ocean, at the circular motion of the stars, and yet they pass by themselves without wondering."

It's never too late to start wondering . . . and writing it down. Someday, when you're roller-skating around the house, grabbing a drink from the fridge, throwing in a load of laundry, or fixing dinner, reflect on that little adventure. Then, sit down and tell about it in here. You'll be glad you did.

CANON AE1

w/24 m
(wide ang

CAPTURING THE JOURNEY

What lies behind us and what lies before us
are tiny matters compared to what lies within us.
—Oliver Wendell Holmes

PART 1

{ 1 }

How do you define adventure?

What does it mean to you to live an adventuresome life?

{ 2 }

"Mother's thoughts were 'close to home,' while Daddy thought 'far away.'
She kept my feet on the ground and he helped me dream." When you
think of "close to home," what comes to mind? When you think of
"far away," what do you dream of and hope for?

What happened today or recently that you loved and want to remember always?

If I were to encourage kids with a simple message
today regarding their childhood, it would be to write things down,
even things that are bad or difficult.

Learn something new while having a good time.

{ 5 }

We are each a combination of many factors woven together out of the joys and sorrows of life. We're the product of our choices. We're the result of what was done for us or to us by our parents. What were the ingredients that made you who you are?

{ 6 }

God creates each of us uniquely by his design and for his purpose.
He readies the path that takes us toward his desired end.

{ 7 }

The world is an enormous place.

Mark the places on this map you'd like to visit and write about why.

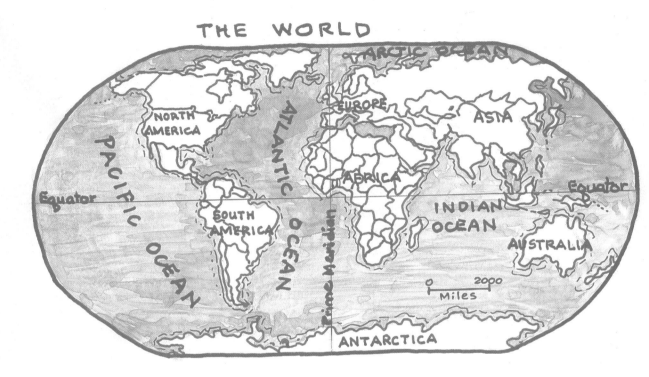

COUNTRY STATISTICS

POPULATION: 984 MILLION
LAND MASS: 1,147,950 SQ MI.
PEOPLE PER SQ MI.: 857
LIFE EXPECTANCY: 61.6 YRS.
LITERACY RATE: 52%
AVG. ANNUAL INCOME: in US $:1,422.?

RELIGION
80%   PROTESTANT: 2%

{ 8 }

No matter what, you have to be yourself!

Don't limit yourself to doing only one thing in life.

Nothing goes to waste in God's economy.

_____

_____

_____

_____

_____

_____

_____

_____

_____

_____

_____

_____

_____

_____

_____

Generally, people do what they want in life if they want it badly enough.

—*Florence Bergendahl*

Negotiate. Laugh at yourself. Quit taking life so seriously. Stop personalizing everything that comes your way. You'll live longer.

Things of value cannot be had for nothing.

What do you value most?

What is the "price" of being true to your own values?

{ 14 }

All serious daring starts within.

—Eudora Welty

We have to spend in order to get and time, money, and energy are our only mediums of exchange. Count on it. Anticipate it and accept it.

{ 16 }

Life has no shortcuts.

Everything starts simply—simple lines, simple thoughts, simple premises.
How would you like to simplify your life? What will you do to get started?

_____

_____

_____

_____

_____

_____

_____

_____

_____

_____

_____

_____

_____

_____

_____

{ 18 }

Adventuresome living is a perspective that touches every part of our being. It's seeing ourselves in relation to the One who created us, the One who gives us courage to face each new day.

_____

_____

_____

_____

_____

_____

_____

_____

_____

_____

_____

_____

_____

_____

_____

_____

_____

There are days when we're so happy our feet don't touch the ground.
Describe a day when your feet didn't touch the ground.

{ 20 }

If I don't dream it and think about it and plan it, nothing will happen.
List your dreams and keep coming back to these pages to fill in your plans.
Make your dreams happen.

You travel over land and sea to win a single convert...

Matt. 23:15

LUCIA DI LAMMERMOOR · LA BOHEME
MEDEA · DAUGHTER OF THE REGIMENT
DON GIOVANNI · SAMSON ET DALILA
MADAMA BUTTERFLY · LA TRAVIATA
ALCINA · PAGLIACCI · ANNA BOLENA
UN BALLO IN MASCHERA · MESSIAH
THAIS · OTELLO · DIDO AND AENEAS
SUOR ANGELICA · ANDREA CHENIER
CORONATION OF POPPEA · MACBETH
JULIUS CAESAR · CARMEN · FIDELIO
AIDA · ORPHEUS IN THE UNDERWORLD
FAERIE QUEEN · NOZZE DI FIGARO
CARMINA BURANA · FEDORA · TOSCA
MERRY WIDOW · COQ D'OR · LA FAVORITA

DALLAS
CIVIC
OPERA
1959 - 1973

The real voyage of discovery consists not in seeking
new landscapes, but in having new eyes.
—*Marcel Proust*

_____

_____

_____

_____

_____

_____

_____

_____

_____

_____

_____

_____

_____

_____

_____

_____

_____

{ 22 }

Given a choice, where do you want to live? Why?

Living a life of adventure may or may not have in it a euphoric
high but it will always have a sense of the unknown.

Never look down to test the ground before taking your next step: only he who keeps his eye fixed on the far horizon will find his right road.

—Dag Hammarskjöld

_____

_____

_____

_____

_____

_____

_____

_____

_____

_____

_____

_____

_____

Adventure starts in the mind then travels to the heart. If it lodges there
long enough, it heads to the ticket counter, gets on a plane, and flies away.
Where have you never been—"out there" or inside—that beckons you?
How can you let the spirit of adventure take you there?

PART 2

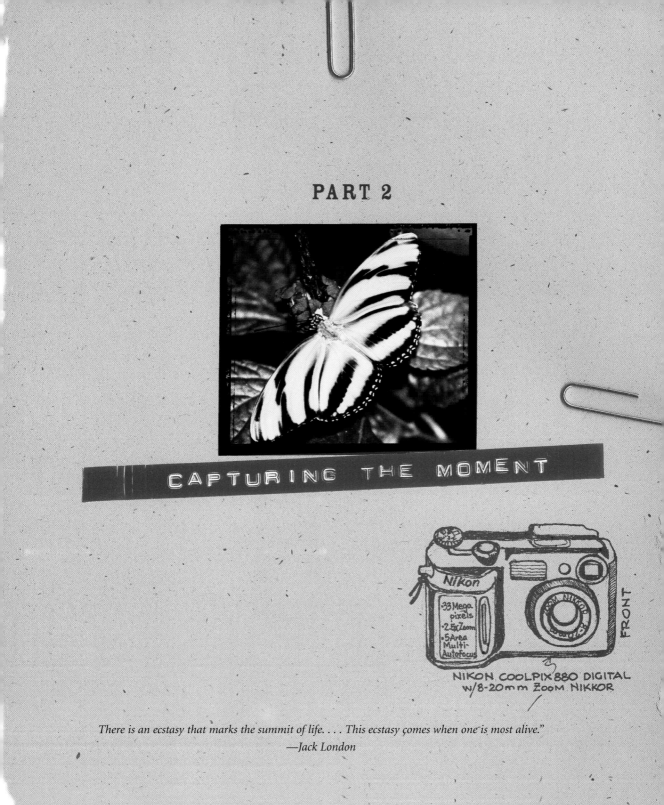

CAPTURING THE MOMENT

NIKON COOLPIX 880 DIGITAL
W/8-20mm ZOOM NIKKOR

Nikon

•3.3 Mega-pixels
•2.5x Zoom
•5 Area Multi-Autofocus

FRONT

There is an ecstasy that marks the summit of life. . . . This ecstasy comes when one is most alive."
—Jack London

{ 26 }

Postcards are the greatest way in the world to capture the moment.
They're colorful, easy to acquire, quick to write, and inexpensive.
Write a postcard to yourself about a favorite moment.

Moments come and go so fast but they are what make up the whole of life. Little bitty moments here and there. They turn into hours and days and weeks . . . ultimately into an entire lifetime.

{ 28 }

Meditation means cultivating a non-judging attitude
toward what comes up in the mind, come what may.

—*John Kabat-Zinn*

*I cried out to God in a letter and told him my fears, regrets,
inadequacies, faultfinding, dread, and despair. Then I wrote this question:
What could I do about it? Write a letter from your heart to God.*

Who are the people in your life who enrich you and make you feel safe and happy?

A safari is the greatest adventure in the world . . . whether it's in Africa
or in the deepest part of your heart. Unexplored landscapes beckon.

Capturing the moment is found in the willingness to go
the extra mile. Describe a time you lived out of this truth.

{ 33 }

Every person who dared to live the life she dreamed started by learning the explosive force of God's lessons. Her soul was liberated from its prison and life began to have genuine meaning.

{ 34 }

Each moment of happiness is only for now. Grab it!

Only that day dawns to which we are awake.
—Henry David Thoreau

Life is full of serendipity. We often plan one thing and, on the way, experience another that's even more interesting, meaningful, or unusual. Describe a time when this happened to you.

_____

_____

_____

_____

_____

_____

_____

_____

_____

_____

_____

_____

_____

_____

_____

{ 36 }

It really doesn't matter where one goes to find adventure in nature.

It lies all around us, in our own backyards and under rocks and trees.

Maybe the thing that causes us to see it easily is that we want to.

Adventure doesn't get any better than this. What do you do that couldn't get any better? What do you dream of doing that would be a great adventure? No dream is too outlandish.

Life is full of serendipitous and surprising detours—
not all of them easily welcomed at the moment.

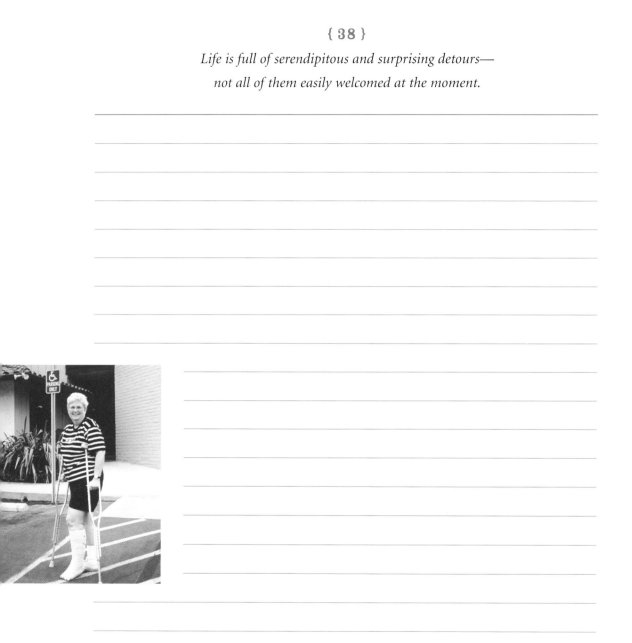

We can respond to challenges and opportunities with "Why not?"
or we can react to reality with "Why me?" It is truly up to us
how we'll encounter what is around the next bend.

MY
KNEE
(possible disorders)

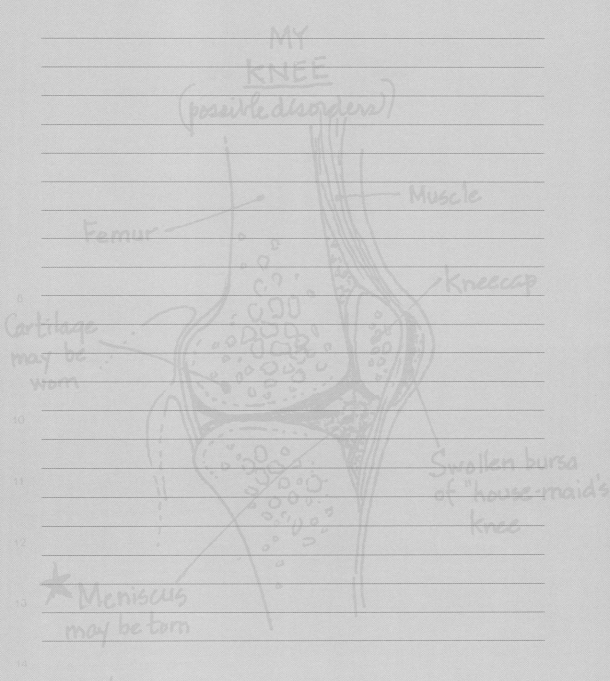

Femur

Muscle

Kneecap

Cartilage
may be
worn

Swollen bursa
of "house-maid's"
knee

★ Meniscus
may be torn

{ 39 }

When we start trusting God outside our comfort zone,
anything can happen, anywhere. Describe a time you trusted
God outside your comfort zone and what happened.

_____

_____

_____

_____

_____

_____

_____

_____

_____

_____

_____

_____

_____

_____

_____

_____

{ 40 }

Drink in life and savor every drop—the sweet and the sour,
the good and the bad, the planned and the unplanned.
When you do, you'll feel fully alive.

Embracing the moment is a choice, a way of life.
It requires us to be awake, mindful of the present.

And when you have reached the mountain top, then you shall begin to climb.

—*Kahlil Gibran*

If only I may grow: firmer, simpler—quieter, warmer.
—Dag Hammarskjöld

{ 44 }

We never know how things will turn out. Live expectantly.

THAT I CALLED UPON THEE : THOU
SAIDST, FEAR NOT."

LAMENTATIONS 3:57

{ 45 }

One thing to remember: with travel, don't take too much.

List ten things you would take on your vacation: a boat trip,

safari, camp, backpacking . . . whatever. Make two columns.

Fill in one column before you leave and the other when you get

back with comments about why that was a good idea or bad.

Never say "never." You have no idea when you might have to eat that word.

Life is crammed with possibilities just on the other side of "never."

"The very things I hated became the making of me."

How true is that for you?

{ 48 }

Make a graph on which you chart your life's journey.

_____

_____

_____

_____

_____

_____

_____

_____

_____

_____

_____

_____

_____

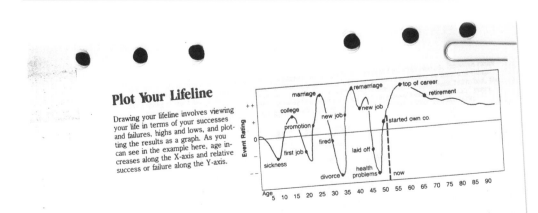

Plot Your Lifeline

Drawing your lifeline involves viewing your life in terms of your successes and failures, highs and lows, and plotting the results as a graph. As you can see in the example here, age increases along the X-axis and relative success or failure along the Y-axis.

From: THE EXECUTIVE FEMALE Magazine
1986 pgs. 31-34

{ 49 }

An upright man gives thought to his ways.

—*Proverbs 21:29*

{ 50 }

One's destination is never a place but rather a new way of looking at things.

—Henry Miller

PART 3

CAPTURING THE LIGHT

We are all teachers and we are all students.
I believe that it is the mark of true wisdom to appreciate and profit from both sides.
—Leo Buscaglia

Imagination should be given freedom to explore the unknown.

If one goes abroad enough, experiences other cultures enough,
sacrifices the comforts of home enough, senses danger enough . . .
one earns an uncertified Ph.D. in High Adventure. One simply
grows and changes. Travel is an education in itself. In what
ways has this proven to be true for you?

Decide things based upon your own viewpoint and experience.

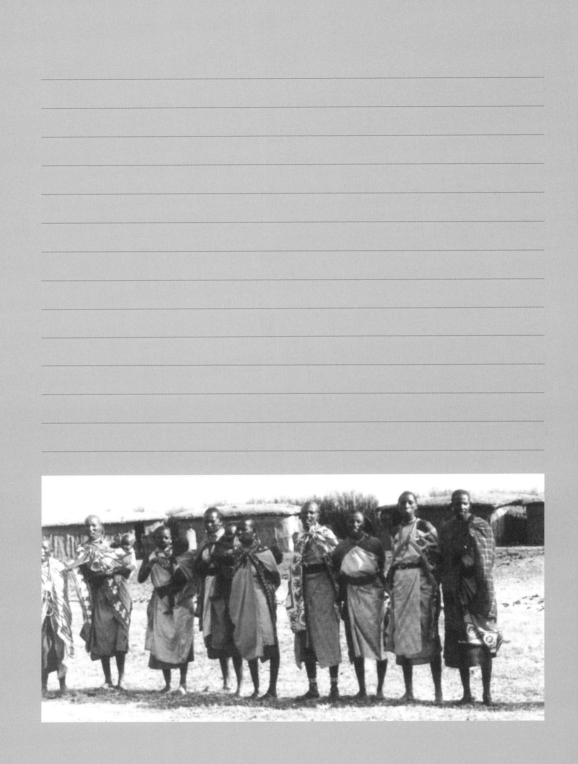

It's important to hold things loosely—relationships, money, possessions, etc.—
because God can always take them away.

_____

_____

_____

_____

_____

_____

_____

_____

_____

_____

_____

_____

_____

_____

_____

_____

_____

_____

The artist is one who looks at life. She's interested and interesting. When a person is interested, she asks herself questions about life. She's curious about her own philosophy. She studies what is in front of her and sees deeper than the outside shell. She wonders. Ponders. Hunts. Turns things over to see what makes them work and of what value they are in the overall scheme of things. And when a person is interesting, she talks about what she has learned in an enjoyable way. What adventures help you capture illumination for your journey?

{ 55 }

Forcing yourself to use restricted means is the sort of restraint that liberates invention.
It obliges you to make a kind of progress that you can't even imagine in advance.

—Pablo Picasso

Enlightened moments provide our greatest happiness or greatest wisdom.

What are your greatest moments of enlightenment? What do they provide for your life?

{ 57 }

When it comes to the field of art, learn to think for yourself.

There is no greater freedom in the world than that of creating something from inside ourselves, unique to us. The artist who never stops experimenting is the one who gives us the most. She dares to create the stuff of her dreams and her daring makes us want to dare as well. Because I was determined my life wouldn't be dull or boring, I wanted to know everything that added quality to everything I did or thought. What do you dare to dream that will make your life richer or more complete? What's keeping you from attempting it? Describe who you are now and who you would like to become.

I shut my eyes in order to see.

—Paul Gauguin

Our friends, on the other hand, went on a walking Safari. The "sanctuary", as they call it here. It's been fun to hear from them every 15 min. or so, through the walkie-talkie. "Baby giraffe...12 o'clock". Or "We're looking straight into the eye of a Bush Buck". They even radioed "we had to lie on the ground to avoid a swarm of bees". BEES? My soul!!!

Anyway, everybody's been enjoying our final day. I've also found time to paint. Such fun. Think I'll try my hand at something else. I'm copying the Timothy Brooke watercolors here in our bungalow. (He's the artist I so loved in the Norfolk).

Boy these are not easy - but so fun to try my hand!.. and to find a place quiet enough to paint and think. Maybe I'm in heaven —

[Someday Luci...many years and many miles from this afternoon, bring it to mind and re-live (the moment. It's now yours for a lifetime) YES!

{ 60 }

Expose yourself to the light around you, opening the
closed doors and windows inside your soul.

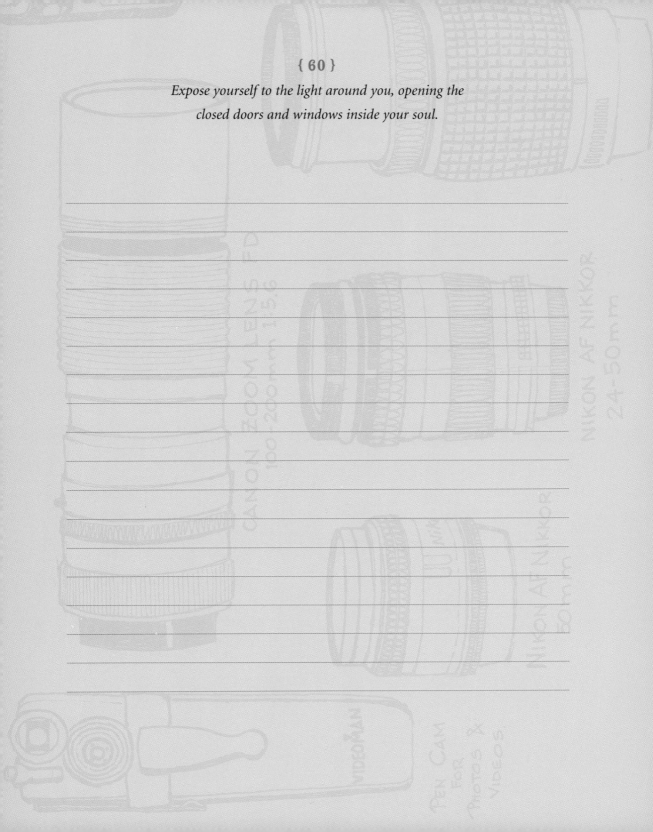

{ 61 }

Art is so much fun. There is nothing about it that is off-putting except our own fear that we're not smart enough to understand it. But . . . we are. We are the recipients of centuries of beauty and bounty that can feed our souls for the whole of our lives, if we just open the door.

THAT'S AFRICA

PHOTO
SIZE 2½" x 3½"

It's important to have fun—to laugh and sing and joke around.

It's important that this kind of spirit permeates our lives and attitudes.

It's important to help others see the humor in their life and circumstances.

It's important to be playful. List at least ten things that are important to you.

*Live fully every moment. If we don't live in this
moment, we'll lose it and it'll never come again.*

If I can get my feelings on paper, it helps me deal with them.

The only way to find your true self is by recklessness and freedom.
—Brenda Ueland

{ 65 }

When we know what we think and why we think it, it gives us richness
in life. What do you know for sure? How does this enrich your life?

This is the victory that has overcome the world, even our faith. Who is it that overcomes the world? Only he who believes that Jesus is the Son of God.

—1 John 5:4–5

This verse sums up the believer's relationship with Christ—we're victors!

If we don't fully live in the moment, there's no rewinding or playing forward that assures us of a better day. But, to live in the moment we have to realize for every good day there's a bad day . . . every zenith has a nadir. If we experience happiness, we're able to do that because we have known sadness. If we experience good health, we enjoy it more having known sickness. The ability to feel anything is based on the degree to which we experience its opposite. What have you learned on a bad day that helped you enjoy a good day?

{ 68 }

*Much about human nature is understandable, forthright, and clear,
but there are things that we'll never understand, no matter how well we get to
know ourselves. How often have you said, "Why in the world did I do that?"
Write about a time you asked yourself that question.*

It doesn't take a lot to make me happy—just the right thing.

What makes you happy?

_____

_____

_____

_____

_____

_____

_____

_____

_____

_____

_____

_____

_____

_____

_____

{ 70 }

How does one remember what happens as the years come and go?

When does one know what is important rather than trivial?

What can one do to keep the memories from fading?

Enjoy friends, life, love, adventure as it's handed to you.

All strong emotion leaves its indelible mark, and it is only a question of discovering how we can get ourselves again attached to it, so that we shall be able to live our lives through from the start.

—*Virginia Woolf*

The most important thing you can ever learn in life is to be able to be alone. Sooner or later the time will come when you will be alone with yourself. You must be able to cope and face your own company.

—Kuki Gallmann

Remember this when journaling: Keep at the initial thing—write.

Only time, experience, and God can change any of us for the better.

The right to live is a matter of essence, not values. In the sight
of God there is no life that is not worth living. . . .
The fact that God is the Creator, Preserver and Redeemer of life
makes even the most wretched life worth living before God
—*Dietrich Bonhoeffer*

PART 4

CAPTURING THE ESSENCE

CANON EOS
w/35-70mm 1:3.5-4.5

How willing am I to be totally myself and what will it cost me?

{ 77 }

The Bible is an amazing volume of work—like no other!

The Bible is the basis for law, order, civilization, and morality.

_____

_____

_____

_____

_____

_____

_____

_____

_____

_____

_____

_____

_____

_____

_____

_____

_____

The Word of God is powerful enough to change
darkness to light and dissatisfaction to joy.
How has God's Word transformed you or your outlook on life?

{ 80 }

Don't manipulate God; just receive. Communion with him isn't something you institute. It's like sleep. You can't make yourself sleep, but you can create the conditions that allow sleep to happen. Create those conditions for receiving God: open your Bible, read it slowly, listen to it, and reflect on it.

—Richard Foster

Where paths that have affinity for each other intersect,
the whole world looks like home, for a time.
—_Hermann Hesse_

What is it about the Bible that catches us off guard . . . that reaches into the depths of our souls and little by little begins straightening us out?

*I do not at all understand the mystery of grace—only that
it meets us where we are but does not leave us where it found us.*
—Anne Lamott

{ 82 }

Not forgiving is like drinking rat poison and then waiting for the rat to die.

—Anne Lamott

_____

_____

_____

_____

_____

_____

_____

_____

_____

_____

_____

_____

_____

_____

_____

_____

_____

Prayer changes us. As we praise God, our burdens lift. As we unload our cares on him, we sense his presence and strengthening. As we confess our sins and wrong attitudes, he forgives us and gives us peace.

{ 84 }

God has promised to meet our needs and he can't go back on that promise.

Start an ongoing list of all the specific ways God meets your needs.

The greater the trust, the wider the blessing. The wider the blessing, the sweeter the joy.

We need an advocate to go before us as well as run with us. Someone who will fight our battles and cheer us on. Someone who will forgive us and strengthen us for the next task. This person is the Savior, Jesus Christ . . . God and man in one person forever.

God's grace has made me a spiritual millionaire. In what ways is this true for you?

We make a living by what we get—we make a life by what we give.
—*Winston Churchill*

{ 89 }

God knows. He loves. He plans ahead.

I want to be a citizen of the world, not just Texas or California or the USA.
I'd like my heart to reach out to all kinds of people, cultures, and ideas.
It doesn't mean I will embrace or believe everything I encounter, but I do want
to know about it and feel comfortable learning.

Nothing is wasted. The good, the bad, the ugly, and the things we think will kill us. God uses it all, and he develops our purpose out of the stuff in our trash. He sifts through it, shows us how to tell it, and then helps others with it. We all meet in our own humanity.

How has God enriched you to help others?

When we ask ourselves hypothetical questions, we, in effect,
reestablish who we are and validate the fact that it's OK to be ourselves.

Learning to be content is an educational process just like all learning. It takes time.

_____

_____

_____

_____

_____

_____

_____

_____

_____

_____

_____

_____

_____

_____

_____

_____

_____

_____

When my heart condemns me and cries, "You have done it again," I am to
believe God again as to the value of the finished work of Jesus Christ.
—Francis Schaeffer

{ 94 }

Allow God's incorruptible truth to become the protoplasm of your soul.
Without doubt he will make a way for you to be truly yourself—apart from having
anybody else in your life. You will grow in him when you rely on what he says.

{ 95 }

If your faith doesn't work when the chips are down
and you never use it . . . what good is it anyway?
—Florence Bergendahl

{ 96 }

When we look at ourselves as the constant recipients of the continual grace
and goodness of God the Father, how can we overdo in giving to others?

{ 97 }

"For you know the grace of our Lord Jesus Christ, that though he was rich,
yet for your sakes he became poor, so that you through his poverty might become rich.

—2 Corinthians 8:9

The future is an open book and the limitations are only in our minds.

{ 99 }

We don't give because it all belongs to the Lord, we give because we've been given to.

—Os Guinness

{ 100 }

The very best way to face tomorrow is to Fear Not. We know who holds our tomorrows.

_____

_____

_____

_____

_____

_____

_____

_____

_____

_____

_____

_____

_____

_____

_____

PART 5

NIKON NUVIS S
w/ZOOM LENS...
22.5-66mm M

CAPTURING THE POSSIBILITIES

The more the years go by, the less I know. But if you give explanations and understand everything,
then nothing can happen. What helps me go forward is that I stay receptive.
—Anouk Aimée

{ 101 }

Thought-provoking questions turn my crank.

What is the stuff your dreams are made of ?

If you had your life to do over, would you do things differently?

The ability to think is a wonderful gift. We take it for granted, yet what would it be like if we couldn't remember, evaluate, determine, make plans, decide right from wrong, or change our minds?

What are the things in life you cannot imagine living without?

_____

_____

_____

_____

_____

_____

_____

_____

_____

_____

_____

_____

_____

_____

Follow your instincts. That's where true wisdom manifests itself.
                                                    —Oprah Winfrey

Imagination is the highest kite one can fly.
—Lauren Bacall

As we grow older, the more frequently we look back in remembrance.

The way to have few regrets is to keep short accounts.

{ 110 }

Think about all the ways God has brought you through life—
adventures, straights and narrows, good times and bad—and how
he has continually cared for you. Write about those times.

_____

_____

_____

_____

_____

_____

_____

_____

_____

_____

_____

_____

_____

_____

_____

Embrace Life as an Adventure

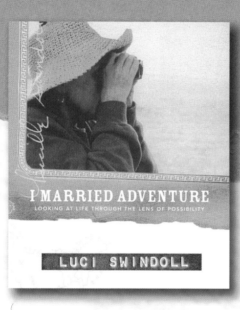

Join Luci Swindoll in the companion full-color book, *I Married Adventure,* for a fascinating tour of a life lived with purpose and passion, one in which she has chosen to "marry" adventure. In this delightful book, Luci shares inspiring stories of her own adventures, highlighted with personal photos, mementos, and artistic sketches. With irresistible enthusiasm, she encourages you to let go of your regrets and celebrate life!

W PUBLISHING GROUP™